CUR

To Morb & Mary Lou
Best Wishes, Chor

CUR

MARTIN MALONE

[illegible] 6/10/15.

Shoestring Press

Printed by imprintdigital
Upton Pyne, Exeter
www.imprintdigital.net

Typeset by narrator
www.narrator.me.uk
info@narrator.me.uk
033 022 300 39

Published by Shoestring Press
19 Devonshire Avenue, Beeston, Nottingham, NG9 1BS
(0115) 925 1827
www.shoestringpress.co.uk

First published 2015

ISBN 978-1-910323-28-1

ACKNOWLEDGEMENTS

Acknowledgements are due to the following publications, anthologies and online journals in which these poems, or versions of them, first appeared: *Acumen*, *Agenda*, *And Other Poems*, *Angle*, *Antiphon*, *Bare Fiction*, *The Black Light Engine Room*, *Boscombe Revolution*, *Cake*, *Dream Catcher*, *Eborakon*, *Elbow Room*, *The Frogmore Papers*, *The Galway Review*, *Hinterland*, *Ink Sweat & Tears*, *The Interpreter's House*, *Iota*, *London Grip*, *Magma*, *The Morning Star*, The *Moth*, *Nutshell*, *Nutshells & Nuggets*, *Obsessed With Pipework*, *Orbis*, *Poetry Ireland Review*, *Poetry Salzburg Review*, *The Poets' Republic*, *PORT*, *Prole*, *The Reader*, *The SHOp*, *Smiths Knoll*, *Stand*, *Thunk*, and *Under The Radar*. Also: the *Vanguard Editions #1 Poetry Anthology*, *'The Ecchoing Green': poems inspired by William Blake*, the *Crystal Clear Voices Anthology*, *The SorgenKind Press 'Matters of the Mind' Anthology* and the *York Literature Festival*, *Mirehouse* and *New Writing Cumbria* websites.

Mrs. Mounter was the winner of the 2012 Mirehouse Poetry Competition. *On An Afternoon Like This She Takes A New Lover* was runner-up in the 2014 Prole Laureate Competition. *Truman On Ischia* was commended in the Frogmore Poetry Prize 2014, *Small Lightnings* was commended in the York Literature Festival Competition 2014. *Eclogue* was shortlisted for the Bridport Prize 2012. Some of these poems constituted the shorter sequence of *Cur*, which was runner-up in the Poetry School/Pighog Press Pamphlet Competition 2013.

Thanks to: Simon Armitage, Paul Batchelor, Jo Bell, Vega Brennan, Brewery Poets, Helen Dunmore, Mark Eitzel, Karen Gleave, Vona Groarke, Alex & Sharon Kirichenko, Charles Lauder Jnr., John Lucas, Michael Symmons Roberts, Jenn Shaw, Hilda Sheehan and Richard Skinner. Thanks are also due to the *Heinrich Böll Association* for a residency in Böll's cottage on the wild and lovely Achill Island, County Mayo.

For Fionn, my Inkling

CONTENTS

"Art is the means we have of undoing the damage
of haste. It's what everything else isn't."
– *Theodore Roethke*

CUR

A tipping point of sorts;
dress it as watershed, crossroads or crest
but we hurl ourselves

downhill

into the fuck of it:
arse over tit,
cock, mouth and clicket.

That point which snuffs out tenderness
with need – ragged and drooling – stinks out
the den with sweat, juice and focus.

In the coop we take more than we need,
delight in the ease of our carnage;
so do with me.

The pack is hard by,
famished with intent.

COLLABORATIONS

This has been coming for weeks,
from that first wink, through the slow
undressing of e-mail to you now here
on my front step, naked but for clothes.
Within seconds we set to, you hitching
your skirt to straddle me on the couch,
me pulling your hips to the biting point.
If we're going to write this book,
we'd best conduct some research.
You roll to one side and get to work
on my flies. I slide the catch of your breath
down the warm slick that soaks through
your pants. Can't be certain but I think I say
that all my birthdays have come at once.
Taking over, you strip me like I'm your infant
and lay me back to watch you lift your shirt,
unhook your bra, and slip free of the skirt.
Gentle tongue you say as you face the other way
and back toward my mouth; assured, specific.
It's soon to become my favourite thing:
the pale, pink-slashed fruit with its dark bud,
the sopping wet fig of you. And these sharp
guzzled toasts to our collaboration.

TUGMAN'S HITCH

Take a single
or round turn
about the post.

Pass a bight
            under the standing part,
then drop the bight
      – your hand guides mine –
over the top of the post.

The beauty of the hitch, you say,
is that it can be let go under load
and yet holds well.

An old working boat friction knot,
a multi-purpose cure-all.

We experiment: first you, then me.

By nightfall
I'm getting the hang of this.

When you pull the spike out,
around two,
      the rope drops off
and the knot unravels.

At dawn
you slip
your moorings.

CHECK-IN

And when we fell into that lobby, the concierge
smelled a rat then judged us by our baggage.

The chankle of chains, a whisper of feathers,
mini-bar well-stocked with ex-lovers,

all tipped her off: we were there to stay.
The bed slept all day, breakfasts lay

uneaten, coffee – one sugar – unstirred
and, as instructed, they did not disturb.

At noon on the third day, our talons raw
with road-kill and the carrion of each other,

we hovered, mid-havoc, when we heard
her at the door backing slowly away.

LOVERS IN AN UPSTAIRS ROOM

After Utamaro

His tongue speaks out the poem of me,
mouthed upon my pillow of down.
Oystercatcher; *Hamaguri ni*
Hashi o shikka to.

O, those hours in the pleasure quarter
when we re-write the *gō* of us, loosen
my *hiyoku*, give flesh its reason.

And on that Autumn evening
when he cannot fly away, we give
and give and gift ourselves allowing.

Thew, kiss, thigh, lips; his heft
upon me, teeth at my nape,
small lightning from breast to cleft.

Unutterable spoken as caress;
unsayable murmured in his melt
and melt, once more into me.

That bud of me found beneath my silk,
the stock of him, planted deep.
This now, this Autumn gives skin its season.

Oystercatcher; *beak caught*
firmly in the clam shell.
His eyes seek out the leaves of me
spread before the wind.

ECLOGUE

Anything from a polecat to a dryad
could be stepping from this wood
into Tuesday light but it is you,
ten years back down the Ridgeway path.
Hitching up those jeans, you reach to take
my hand, palm off doubt, knuckle faith
onto ringless fingers. This isn't you
– this feral stuff – low impulse being
more my thing but that day you push me
up against a tree as old as Silbury.
We emerge from the thicket-gloom aglow
with escape and getting away with it;
it an as-yet indeterminate: some fuzzy
co-ordinate on a half-sketched map.

Today I stick to the downland track
skirting the spot, though stop to look.
Anything from a polecat to a dryad
could be stepping from the wood
into this light but it was you,
among the things I could not see.

ALICE

I give you this, my snow-and-blackthorn heartland
and its morning heron in the beck,
my Viking Lyvennet with its boltwood bridge.

The water pools darkly on the weir's brow,
down the fish-bridge chicanes
a rill, subtle as lamprey.

Fanged with ice, the bank's mossy walrus
talks to me of many things: our last-nights
and mornings, your dawn-lit flesh and sleep.

Sleep on while I bend to pluck these stems:
cold ivory from which to carve a chess set,
frore gimlets with which to plant a kiss.

Then you're beside me, in a wind-tumbled
fluster of rooks and their cracked peppercorn
of song. My gift you take upon your lips,

kiss fingers back to life,
tease summer from the ice.

LIFE DRAWING

Sunlight solders the morning into place
mote-by-mote; lasered almost to portrait:
you as *Still Life*, you as *Reclining Nude*.
Yes, let's play this game and go there,
leaf through your back pages, trace the stages
and versions that led you to now and this man
watching you sleep; armed only with guesswork
and the little he knows.

Were he a gambler, he'd stake good money
on a bonny child, long of limb and happy
as an elver in its quicksilver.
Always glad, always grasping delight, you stomp
before him in the rock-pools of a hometown beach,
Daddy in tow, black-and-white and last century.

Were he a surgeon, he'd size up the scar
above your brow, begotten of drink
and a wrong 'un boyfriend. Were he *clairvoyant*,
the man might see beyond your sleeping form
into random dreams with the running-dog
euphoria of fields and unleashed love.

But here he stands in the early light, drawing
together some sense of your life before
you met; sketching outline and general form,
exercising the privilege of transposition:
one year moved to the next, connectedness
given to isolated stones, lone trees granted
hillsides. Some capture of hinterland,
an inkling shade of unknown.

SPOIL

Scrabbling around in trenches, trying to find
the Great Seal you tossed into that now dried-up
river bed, some days – a glimpse maybe – I think

I see it half-sticking out of the render
of a parapet's ghost or some midden's
pick-up stick of bones and cuttlefish.

Your one big love: that great affair
from the Second Dynasty of your twenties,
the one I sometimes struggle to match.

There was rumour of a trove, a hoard
of lightning struck into coin and relics
of your one true god; though it yielded

little, the enigma of your sands safe
among the pottery and biofacts,
looted, perhaps, by that guy who hit you.

I watch you sleep, toy with calling in
the experts – perhaps some diviner
of your heart – though none, of course, exist.

Likely, I've been looking in the wrong place;
nothing for it, then, but to trust my eyes,
take my time and slowly dig.

MARTINS

We stopped ourselves to watch the nestlings return
to the village and this bedroom window.
Like all migrants they were out of the loop,
having missed those winter storms that dashed
their wattle cup of home onto the garden below.
You drove in deep under the eaves of my shoulder,
whispered something about homecomings
and wondered if they'd try to rebuild.

All that week we spent in bed, ourselves
nesting into snug futures lined with feathers,
forget-me-nots, your everywhere-red hair.
And the martins' will gave out; their niche remained
a coffee-stain ring of mud at the frame's corner,
liminal as your Tuesday check-in.

CHICAGO

After nine years married to a German
you had learned his words for *slug*, *story*
and *squirrel*. I arrive at The Bean early,
take in the mix of Anish Kapoor and downtown,
then step back to watch you from the crowd.

From behind a bush and through the huddle
of escorted Japanese, what I see is your ease;
this cool of you, that could follow
your husband so far from home but keep back
enough leisure to let slide his mother tongue.

Your smile is at home here in this adopted city,
your form comfortable with its warped reflection
in the Cloud Gate's quicksilver. Behind me,
Lake Michigan crouches beyond Millenium Park,
and the Plaza's possibility of mirage.

When I *Hey presto!* myself through the arch,
my arm slips around you on a spot called the *omphalos*,
a fact I swear is coincidence. We wrap ourselves
in the hundred silver manifolds of us,
a thousand *geschichten* to learn or let slide.

DOING WORDS

Craughing [craff - ing]
Verb, compound *craughing,* synthesis: *laughing* + *crying* / a simultaneous mixture of laughing and crying/ reflection of melancholic joy or longing/ synonymous roots: *cianail* (Gael), *hiraeth (Welsh), duende (Sp), schwermut* (Ger) etc.

That morning we invented a verb; our own
for the mixture of laughter with tears.
We kept the curtains closed, skedaddled the phone

and shut out what had been our L-Train year.
Your dog overheard, broke into the room,
storming the broken old bed, licked our ears

till we could see the bigger picture loom:
us, this city, some future and his walk.
Out on the corner of Argyle and Bloom,

I saw my first fireflies. We stopped to talk
to some Mexican neighbours who thanked
you for watering plants when they went to New York.

Back here in the east Cumbrian dank,
I pop into town to pay bills and send you
this; *craughing* all the way to the bank.

LIKE I WAS YOUR GIRLFRIEND

Afterwards, I step out into the yard,
shaking the silver from your jumper,
the punkish one I bought when last home.

And now we've completed the look:
you are John Lydon, a young Strummer,
you are your son, the spit of me.

When you put your glasses on, we are
both your grandfather, Bobby, shorn
back to life by my ham-fisted razor.

Handing you your wig, I try on heartache
for size but it no more fits this evening than
the day when, aged four, I wore your hat.

We laugh at your new cut – it takes years
off you – but most of all we are relieved
you carry it off, deep in your bones.

BUTCH & SUNDANCE RIDE BACK INTO TOWN

That moment when I start to learn to bend:
man at the wheel of his milk-float, round done
and about to get back to the depot, son
riding shot-gun to pay for his new bike.

Then Dad goes outlaw on me, turns in
a lifetime of solid adherence, turtles
his shell of honest-John, hands back
his Sheriff's badge, joins the James Gang.

We are backing up by the Dutch Houses
when the bang jolts us. Fistful of dollars,
we've been bushwhacked. Gold top bounces
from its crate and smashes onto pavement.

The toppled-brick gatepost, an instant
of recognition, some blue spark of decision:
head for the hills or hands-up confession?
Father, model for me what is right

or show me a different way. *Drive, DRIVE!*
Heavy on the reins, alias Smith and Jones,
deep in the saddle and the one thing
we've got to get is out of this business.

You can't touch him for it, he's gone; jumped in
the river before me, caught that paddle-boat.
I am twelve and I'm driving the milk-float
back into town. We are laughing all the way.

EGGING

The hedgerow was Dad's cashpoint; from it
he'd casually withdraw the small currencies
of wonder: my first finch egg, sheep skulls,
an old wren's nest, the dunnock's four-way
clutch of blue.
            Slum-cleared city kid,
he had ranged the estate margins into edgelands
to forage new-found greenery; suck marrow
from deciduous bones, lap time like stolen cream.
What he really handed me was some final flourish
of golden-summer cliché, out-of-step with these times.
No point, then, but the passing-on of breakable things.

LORDS OF THE RING

Now that was a world order Aunt Norah
could understand: fat lads and uncles tucked
into spandex, proving nimble with Saturdays.
While East and West faced off, the big boys
got to grips in some grunting town hall.

Warrenpoint and moonwalks were nothing to her,
so long as Dickie Davies rolled up
with his *Mallen* streak and kipper tie;
glint in his eye and tache well-groomed.
He can light up any room, that lad, said
she on her knees beside the grate.

Giant Haystacks got her riled when, behind
the referee's back, he leathered Leon Arras
the Man from Paris, though that was nothing
to her scorn for Harvey Smith or the way
Pat Roach knocked out The Nature Boy.

While '77 was The Pistols and Jubilee,
for me it was the sight of Norah
tearing raw meat from the telly as
Big Daddy unmasked Kendo Nagasaki:
Do him Shirley! He's a nasty bugger!

What she liked was how Les Kellett always
seemed out-on-his-feet but managed to win,
the way Catweazle tickled Mick McManus
into submission and a distant sadness
in the lost blue eyes of Jackie Pallo.

GADD'S OWL

Autistic as the day is long; to us pre-decimals
he was *nutjob, loony,* and *spazz.* While
Miss Tobin tried to explain new pence,
Old Bug-Eyes moaned like a revving Cortina,
chewed on his carpus when he got upset,
or unsure. That bloody, corned-beef wrist,
gnawed-at and angry as a gypsy's curse.

Round-headed and squat and commonly found
in the playing field scrub we called The Wood,
he was the last of our worm-eaters; swallowed
them whole to delight the girls, showed his own
to make them squeal. Kewicking, scratching
and kicking, he was fierce in defence
of his polythene den beside the railings.

Impossible to withhold comment, then,
on the ironies of choice made
when a crippled Tawny took to roosting
in the garage of the Gadd's semi. Why there
in Hart Station, so far from his twisted oak?
Perhaps old *Stix* sensed a kindred varmint
or deciphered the house name's Latin. Maybe.

Things ended grimly at *Stella Maris.*
Gadd's owl, grown tired of celebrity, tried
a return to the bole before he was ready.
Like a tidal grounding, we gathered
to help but saw him beaten each time,
as he flung himself from his perch
into the metal door with a *doom, DOOM…*

Christopher's Dad did what was right: to our
sickened delight he banjaxed his Brown Owl
with a tent pole. Collectors to a man,
we fell upon the carrion, stripping it
down for parts. I took a talon for some grim
work with a knife. Yet on my desk, it is
school again. And again that bloody wrist.

OLD YHA HANDBOOKS

Readable now for their litany of lost names:
Arnside, Bridport, Aysgarth Falls, the castle
at Ferniehurst – with its mad old warden –
Westerdale Hall. And that moorland slog

to be turned away at Wheeldale; with Frank,
having failed to phone ahead and us judged
to be motorists and so low priority.

I once spent a night in Kielder before it slipped
below the lake and a week at Penmaenmawr
while we fell apart. A weekend at Bala
with Dad and cousin Joe yielded Kodacolor

prints of his early gut and my first-time
Adidas stripes. Others were gone before
we even started: Dirt Pot, Gretna, Holt.

Aliases were for locals or the hard-core;
so, Buntingford, Corris and Eastbourne
were lesser known as Wayside, Ratgoed
and Beachy Head. And some, it would seem,

never rose from the page: Hunstanton,
Battle and Draethen were all listed; though doors
never opened and Drying Rooms grew cold.

Mine from '75, with its olive green cover,
and overnights of 45p-to-a-pound, I found
in my Mother's bottom draw; kept as proof
of my childhood. Also saved: the hostel stamps

– once coveted like duelling scars – and that green
enamel triangle, later pinned to a first guitar strap.

One day, I joined for life and never went back.

HAND-PAINTED TRUNK FROM YEMEN, 1989

For the most part, I like to keep my trap shut,
say nothing to anyone, containing myself.

These crude studs, securing the flap of my lock,
pin me down to a decorative silence and perhaps

that is best, for my Greek cousin spoke only havoc.
I am – forgive me – a girl of the harem

hand-painted in henna swirls, decorated
to please yet functional: a deep-throated

skill of accommodation one of my principal
charms, the reason, even, for you to emirate

yourself and pluck me from among my sisters
here on this shelf in the Old Town souk.

Hire a porter to wheel my wedding carriage
through these dusty backstreets and dead-chicken

alleys, then sing me devotional songs
across this three-lane highway to your palace.

EGYPTOLOGY

This walk
toward a lack of things,
the valley, itself a rocky sump of air,
harboring little but a laid-off name.

In search of it
we duck the midday heat
for beetle-black, hauling our sun
down the humid passageway
of KV34.

Progress is not easy:
onset with a stairway
then corridor, another stairway;
a second corridor and ritual shaft
where the Isis-blue
skies a mess of stars.

Grave robbers
took their ninety-degree turn
into the vestibule
with the gods still warm,
when our century caught up
even the mummy had gone.

Here then,
the oval chamber,
a red quartz sarcophagus
– its graved outline of absence –
and the name, Tuthmosis.

Months later,
when you fire up the kiln
and put my head in it,
you risk that crucial thing,
the lingering trace of water
which blows the egg of my skull
to this, another lack.

WOOD ON THE DOWNS

After Paul Nash

We have been here before. Uffington, Hackpen,
Grim's Ditch, Ogbourne St.George, Wayland's Smithy,
Sparshott Firs, Bishopstone and Barbury;
all the trodden way from Overton
to Beacon Hill. Each place its *genius loci*,
a favourite colour: Ash-Blue, Ochre,
Payne's Grey, Terra-Verte, Lamp Black, Sienna.
But today you ditch your winter tones
and bid for late spring. The trees are in leaf,
chalk from the downland reflects light
from a milder sky. *Through field glasses*
one sees a landscape that one can see
in no other way. Here, then, is yours:
the stiff cilia of trunks – a brown-fringed
platoon lost on Hill 60 – ghosts of the vortex,
the leaching colours of pending summer,
the breast, lumbar and hip curve of hill
prone upon the bed of Buckinghamshire.
And there I join you eighty years away
with my Trojan girl; lifting her face
to mine in the dappled light of the wood.
We have been here before.

HOUSE BY THE RAILROAD

It was all about parallels, that house
on Ocean Road: running lines laddering
the level gust of coastal track,
those vertical shafts of Doric column,
the long tracking shot of its upstairs lounge
that held on the North Sea's horizon.
And that little life with mine, waving back
at me from the attic room which never
opened, as I crossed the bridge to the Dene;
from there to the shore and on out to sea.

MONT SAINTE-VICTOIRE

Cézanne as Sisyphus: each day climbing
the steep sides of self, a mountain on his back,

to lose the light, to not quite get right the it,
the it-of-it. Rolling back down him each night

toward the morning; a mountain on his back,
each day climbing: Cézanne as Sisyphus.

HELEN AND ERIC

After Eric Ravilious

Some showery Spring Tuesday not long from war,
rise early, shave, pack a flask, the *Shell Guide*
and your box of watercolours. A last quick
Brylcreem slick in the hall mirror, Tirzah's kiss
and the grudging chug of an Austin engine
fades around *Furlongs* as you leave to conjure
Uffington. The light's not promising and
forecast storms could bring grief: too wet
and watercolour will pool, buckling the page;
accident-prone to the last, it reacts badly to raindrops.
We make good time through Hampshire
and the back lanes of Berkshire;
reach the Vale of the White Horse by noon,
labouring up beyond the Betjemans
at Garrard's Farm to park in a lay-by
below Dragon Hill.

Here's not quite right,
something lower suits you more. As if shy
of the full-on wholeness of horse, you walk
away, using the Ridgeway's depth, its longer
aspect, askance light. Muralist by trade,
you now have your great wall of sky and turf,
with its scoured earth-cut of chalk. This you do
understand. The cross-hatch of grass, a nail-bed
of wheat stalks, the shifting pools of thin light,
striations of green hillside frail of contour
against pale line. The late retrospective has
an *almost nothing*, a *see-through dream starting
in reality and ending in its own radiant
elsewhere*. Work done, you pack away your stuff
and we head for home.

MRS. MOUNTER, CIRCA. 1914

You have seen them come and go: the salesmen,
stevedores, undergraduates and tinkers,
lorn veterans of Omdurman and Colenso,
the struggling artist with his curious hours;
all passing through the widow's breach of spare
room. Your years lived impasto – caked-on,
palpable as Sunday Best – are rendered boldly,
dealing only in certainty, creed and nation,
dealing solidly in bricks and mortar
and the definite vertical of the doorway
that frames you as you sit, impassive
as the teapot, immovable as the rent.
Outside the world turns to mud, feeds its sons
to fire and lead and names you will hear
for the first time: *Passchendaele, Somme, Ypres, Mons….*

PENSIVE HEAD

After Wyndham Lewis

What is it about that Thirties palette?
Those browns, a decade-long autumn endlessly
taking leave of the branch: stoic farewells
on steam-swamped platforms, pensive heads
opaque through café windows; ducking down
to order soup through hatches, fingers like
rheumatic sausages prop sallow faces
bent over the tea cup of thwarted lives.
As if the brush knew what was coming,
as if it hunkers down in the spectrum's
trench: a reflex wrapped in khaki, nurtured
in mud and want. Of eyes that have witnessed
too much; that have seen the peacock's head
held under Brown Windsor, shot off above
the parapet of, say, ochre. At the quayside
dirty hankies wave goodbye to the red
neckerchiefs bound for Aragon, stand back
to let the tanks pass, wave through the ranks
of goose-stepping shirts; yes, those shirts.

PRESENCE OF MIND

After Magritte

You always were the patsy, heavy-lidded,
fish-mouthed: an outsider on his perch.
Falconmanfish, quicksilver of scale,
sharp of suit and tail feather.

Did they trust your trinity? In the
zoo you were loved and triple-fed.
The school trips, coach-loads and family
groups gawping at your indecision.

When they let you out to roam the streets,
at what crossroads were you given a *genus*?
Walk/Don't Walk, Fly/Don't Fly, Swim.
Your unique agony of choice.

From the Book Depository window, a view:
the river, a street and vault of sky.
My god, they've shot the President!
The knoll's talon, fin and thin black tie.

FIGURE WITH RAISED ARM

Untitled moments:
a million in one lifetime;

this the Travolta dance, tribal surrender,
or tube train standing anchor,

that convinced wave to the stranger
you thought an old friend, half-cousin, ex-lover

– part of you blushing already at the error
you'll recount when next you meet them for real –

or the hip-cocked hailing of the cab
that does not draw up beside you,

nor ever stops on its way downtown.

GHOST OF A GENIUS

"First of all the art of living", Paul Klee

Black smudges
where his hand
rested
on the paper
give it away:
stitches of moment,
breath-frosted glass.

All genius
is puppetry.
Time, disease and early death
– the string-pulling fingers –
dance duration
down a path to eternity.

Take away the ghost
and you have what it is.
Large eyes, cropped beard,
the tilted, domed head,
arms flopping down
under the weight of fatherhood:
a toy for Felix Paul.

His masterpiece.

PIAZZA

After Giacometti

Seven AM in *Piazza Plebescito*,
not the human figure but long shadows
cast in this bronze light of April morning.
Freeze the frame. Bookshop owner opening
up on *Piazza Dante*, the Crib Street
assistant with her new lover to meet,
a Mergellina fisherman dropping
off fresh *vongole*, the Vomero lawyer
and Caremar sailor bound for Ischia:
ghosts of the unreal city, thin as nails.

He'd make your head look like the blade of a knife.

UNTITLED

Translation after Pierre Jean Jouve

The man who'll be dead tomorrow
may die no more today.
He'll listen to his heart beating
in the immensity of his flesh;
and the million blue suns
that can gild a single night
are not beyond his hopes.

Unable to recall what it's like
to have never killed a man,
could he, himself, be dead,
breathing deep the darkness?

ARCHIVES

After Christian Boltanski

We are all so complicated,
then die;
from one stage pass quickly
to the next, become
objects that were someone.

The eye seeks out pattern and is satisfied.
What can you see
in a darkened room:
ten columns of three,
saints' bones for the century?

Each one has his own life,
each her own story:
the children of Dijon,
unknown person,
stolen graduates of Vienna.

Into every eye shines a light,
its wires trailing clumsily
down the wall,
and beneath each face
a tin box for the soul.

BEE DRESS

She came back from Dubai with nothing to wear;
Paris, Fifth Avenue, London, Rome now this.
One week from the wedding and my lover
was sullen, ill-at-ease, waxing nervous.

Not my credit card nor blind devotion,
neither *haute couture* nor catwalk shows,
not *Gaultier, Versace* or *McQueen*: none
could raise the bloom on my English rose.

Gardener's Question Time gave me 'Five To Try':
Ragged Robin, Red Campion, Cowslip,
Sorrel and, the lovers' favourite, Ox-eye.
Though it was bees I sought, not blooms to clip.

I know my Classics, bee women are best,
Zeus saves them for the lucky man
and I like to think I'd pass that test.
So, on my grandmother's *Singer*, I ran

her up a dress of honeybees, cotton
and wax. Tailoring for symmetry,
I scoured the wood for man-styled blossoms
and stitched up a nettle jacket for me.

She wasn't happy. As a dressmaker,
it seems, I leave a lot to be desired.
The nap prickled this way and that, contour,
line, bodice and bust were all *passé* or tired.

But the local High Street offered nothing
and her designer had moved to Nepal.
The events manager, not wishing
to panic her, thought it might work after all.

So the girl had her big fat wedding day,
looked stunning in honeybees, best-pleased
that Daddy was well enough to give her away:
the paid-for fairy-tale, until she had to leave.

I'll resist the obvious pun. Some say
it was the nectar or voice of the hive,
but she threw skyward her bridal bouquet
and was gone, nevermore to be seen alive.

Twelve months later, I married the bridesmaid,
her sweet-tempered sister, who favoured jeans
and baggy jumpers. We have four great kids,
no need to dress-up, if you know what I mean.

SEVEN STRANGERS

I *Bespoke*

Strangest among them was a crying man,
spectacles dangling from a chubby paw,
trousers rolled like a mason; webbed feet
plodging in the shallows of a bleak shore.

For no reason I could discern, he was
crying, there in his Saville Row suit.
Said it was bespoke, like each of his waves.
Said he was a Titan robbed of his powers.

II *Flesh*

Rolls of fat, beautiful, a lazy tumble
of tuck and bulge; she earthed the world's balloon
in a landscape I thought I'd seen before,
knew from somewhere: a place born of places.

Not the fetish flesh of baby cheeks,
mother-loved and easy, not the ripped skin
of finch carcass, headless, torn and spent,
nor lovers' trim hide, no, something different.

III *The King*

Easy to overlook, he lay for weeks
in a loose foetal: Saxon bones,
a child's pet alien. I only saw him
because of boredom and an idle minute.

He pulls together the grave goods of himself,
shakes down the gunk placenta jacket,
tight-focuses his sherry-drunk stare,
looks me up and down then leaves the building.

IV *The Model*

She came to me in a dream, converted
by day into that walk, tick-tocking
a sashay along the old breakwater.
I called out to her, telling her to stop

but she had no ears for the likes of me
no, not when the catfish sat in sports cars
– creamy grins on barbell chops – winking up
at her as she tumbled off those kitten heels.

V *Dancing Shoes*

Retired from the tomcat game, he took
to dance; speaking steps in a register
unfamiliar to these ears. We met in a pub
on the Old Boundary Road, between

the new Tesco and the wasted dockyard.
Talking at cross purposes, we persisted
until eight when pussy arrived and, cheek to cheek,
they waltzed away toward the west.

VI *Cave Canem*

I thought it was a dog, lying there panting
like a good 'un; chest a stink-breath bellows,
tongue lolling downhill to the port. Turns out
it was some joker's idea of love, chained

to the gatepost waiting for the lava flow.
I hadn't the time to hang about – what
with the pyroclastic cloud and all – so
I threw the poor mutt a bone. Loyal though.

VII *Rock*

He wasn't wrong, they really did look something,
that field full of fair folk; E-d up to the nines
and mad for it as the Mondays after
Good, Better, Best. What was he doing there

in some Malvern valley, at the changeover
from blue-eyed soul and new psychedelia
to the Second Summer of Love,
with no reliable guide to the truth?

INFERNO

So, Christopher, when you ask in your metal voice
what Hell is, I shall answer that it's you:

a very other person. So other as to make me
neuro-typical and you wired-up wrong,

to allow me superpowers of everyday nuance
while you struggle to decode my very smile.

Other as in 'different', other as in Minotaur:
that freak-in-the-corner other.

Hell is this secondary school, with its change
of rooms, change of subjects, two-week timetable,

change of changes with each new head.
Hell, Christopher, is here and being you.

And I mean, by that, love.

THE GHOST OF RICHARD III WATCHES 'BLADERUNNER'

Perched on the edge of a tower block,
the battery-tired replicant runs an audit
of his second life. Critically damaged,
his circuits flicker down to a final spark.
It's raining. Heavy drops cast over him
a shroud of white noise as he peers
across the broken city and takes stock.

It is not the giddy collapse of stars,
nor the sucking void of dark matter,
it is not the welted arms of galaxies
nor the dog-like joy of besting gravity.
None of these seize the smart chip
that quickens him into something
approximating life. Only a pall of rain
and through it the pinprick of light
from which he was made.

MEET THE BAND

Drums

The backbeat is all
– triplet, sinew, farts and porn –
born to it, solid.

*

Bass

Cool sociopath,
he locks on tight to the kick
and fingerwalks home.

*

Keys

I'm the doctor's son,
had grade 8 by eleven:
the real musician.

*

Gtr

Band visionary
quotes, verbatim, *Spinal Tap;*
writes all his own stuff.

*

Vox

Iconographer,
my face is our destiny,
dumb-throat history.

NO TIMEWASTERS PLEASE.

BIGMOUTH STRIKES AGAIN

I'm afraid I'm an open book, I say stuff,
confess too readily in my cups and

mess-up in moments like these: you
with your roman nose held high in disgust

at my latest *faux pas*. And, sweetness,
I know you are only half-joking when

you say I should be bludgeoned in my bed
for selling my Smiths ticket so I could

go see The Armoury Show instead.
But, at the time, you were only four

and, having seen them twice before –
like a Beckett play – I felt I'd got the point.

Besides, liking Jobson longer, there was
a seniority of quiff thing to be respected.

Connected was my love for McGeogh's guitar
which I felt might fade out before Marr's.

So don't give me back those mix tapes, don't melt
down my old Walkman; consider it my

legacy to this retro age of legacy,
alongside these inconvenient truths,

my scratched vinyl, your gigsandtours.com.
Because here in old Camden Town,

out drinking with the hung-on-too-long
I sense that I've moved on. Lover, please

stop me if you think that you've heard this one before
and don't make me know how Joan of Arc felt.

I CAN'T EXPLAIN

He has an Irish mother,
a Syrian Dad and likes
the mix. Athan says he's got
chips with everything
and two axes to grind.
As a boy he helped them run
the Kilburn café, serving
the *labneh* and Boxty
through the hot Summer of '76.
That's when he's into Punk,
catches the Pistols early,
sees the Terry Chimes Clash
and buys a Vic Goddard suit.
The Jam he likes best, though,
and, by the time of the Mod Revival,
rides a classic *Lambretta* round town
and down to Brighton in a state
of heightened *Quadrophenia*.
Not even the al-Nusra boys
can talk him out of this one,
nor his passion for The Who.
It's a love that abides
beyond radicalisation
and Wahhabi purism;
in the same way he stared down
the mohawks and art school
fundamentalists when he bought
that scooter. So today he picks out
the classic target tee, shoulders
his *Kalashnikov* and slips out
onto the *Yarmouk* street, blinking
in the glare of the morning sun.
The sniper can't miss.

VER: A MODEST PROPOSAL

"And if you know your history, it's enough to make you heart go oh-oh-oh-oh"
(Terrace song, sung at Everton and Celtic)

Citizens! We are but one syllable from a better world.
Governed by old-Evertonians think how much better we'd fare.
Work with me here, forget the current Cabinet and picture this:
Howard Kendall Prime Minister, Duncan Ferguson his Chief Whip,
and, in Number 11, Kevin Sheedy lines up the tricky Spring budget
like a direct free kick. Venerable Father of the House is Dixie Dean,
while Peter Reid guides communication; his trademark directness
a constant source of privately-educated discomfort.
Duncan McKenzie, ever the entertainer, nutmegs Boris,
then does it again just because he can, the loveable Bertie
landing flat on his wadded arse, gazing up at God-given talent
from some Kensington gutter. Gove simply goes, giving way
to the educated right foot of state-schooled Paul Bracewell.
When a special guest on *Desert Island Discs*, Premier Kendall
makes no pretence of loving early REM, dubstep or The Smiths
in some misguided attempt to get down with the new-vote kids;
preferring instead Sinatra's *My Way* and confessing his regard
for both Rene *and* Renata. In some not-too-distant future, be assured,
the Thirty-Year Rule will not reveal secret plans to crush the unions,
put troops on the streets or close down entire mining communities,
but a rather stylish passing and pressing game that graced our screens,
brought modest success in Europe and two league championships
denied due credit by the Heysal mob. Judicious dealings
in the transfer market keep us ticking over and a ruthlessness
at home means avoiding tricky away trips to remote island groups
in order to stay alive in the competition. For this reason, we welcome
migrant workers who add depth to the squad, rather than dilute
the pool of home-grown talent carefully developed in our academy.
Most of all, we refuse to sell our best weapons to rivals across the park,
who then come back to haunt us in tough away fixtures all over the place.
No shoot-to-kill but 'aving a dig from distance, no appropriation
of the Great War but an honest minute's silence before kick-off.
Unfashionable in Norway and the Far-East, we too struggle to attract

inward investment but, when the boom goes bust, we'll still be here
with our modest means and manageable overdraft. I could go on.
This is not the politics of envy but those of free association,
born of frustration at the state of the nation, no consolation
to the rhyme-heavy slam of the Neo-Toff networks that run us.
People's Club or the Bullingdon. Citizens, the choice is yours.
It's a loose manifesto but I put it to you. Imperfect though better, surely.
Just think about it is all I ask. But, then, we know our history…

SWEENEYS

I forgot, like you, to die:
the blight did not take me
but my brothers and every other.

And then a tupenny crossing
– exhausted, famished for escape –
riding the tide of hunger.

I fell in among the cautious
whose first landfall served enough
to feed five generations.

After starvation their simple stew
seemed to fill my mended boots
and heft my pick enough

to cut a railroad through
the English hills, then dig
your motorways for pittance.

A sign outside the London pubs
shut out my bared shoulders
the day I built your palace.

Another, when bolloxed
and looking for a flop: not blacks,
not dogs nor – least of all – me.

But I forgot, like you, to die:
the blight did not take me
and, one day, I am going home.

TRUMAN ON ISCHIA

The room chooses itself: a writer's space
with a balcony above the harbour,
two chairs, table and a tortured old bed.
Its provenance comes later, as she pours
us Lachrimae Christi and talk turns
to the *buena séra* under a sky of early stars.

I forget why we came here – your sister
perhaps – but here we are in Forio
on Boxing Day in Capote's old room
at the *Pensione de Lustro*, both town
and coincidence as intimate
and satisfying as one's own heartbeat.

Islands are like ships at permanent anchor,
no place for the rush of hours, the dropped watch
an outrageous bit of symbolism to prove
his point. Crossing the tiles, I see Truman
on the balcony as the Virgin comes to town,
forgetting to throw his votive ribbons.

In forty-nine, Signora Mussolini still sat
out her quiet exile in shabby black
and the town's two idiots claimed their island
in the afternoon's white midnight.
Maria watered her drinks, Gioconda awaited
a letter and her spring was the longest ever.

The longest and the loveliest.

RED KITES AT UFFINGTON

The hunting pair stirs
a lazy spoon of air   above the coombe.

Milvus milvus
– imminent as snow in the second before fall –
turning upon
the axis of self.
There.
A reeling this of this,
the element 'I' circling
in a plughole pull of want.

This ground is incidental,
good only for carrion
or missable
drift.

And Sunday stops its junket,
holds still awhile to watch:
red-meat method of vole,
silent drone of shrew,
leveret shock and awe.

Lear's detested daughter
– driven from Tudor parish
for the price on her carcass –
is back
above
the Berkshire Downs
and all the birds of Oxfordshire
and all the birds of Oxfordshire
and all the birds of Oxfordshire…

THAT WINTER

After a month of snow came the rains:
chugging against the tide up Meaburn Edge,
peering through mizzle toward High Cup Nick,
all-but-stalling in lakes on the Reagill road.

The martins' nest grew sodden and heavy;
broke its spittle moorings after the night
of gales, played mud-pies with my bedroom sill
then feasted on the garden table.

Mornings were night-black and blue with cold:
big icicles snottered the gable end,
drive time was lost scraping rime off the car,
while great tits diminished in the hard frost.

The Lyvennet heron, a leggy grey clock,
met me at the gate each day; his fish round,
pulling in at the rock below the weir,
let me know if I was early or late.

Past October, the neighbours went part-time,
became a T.V.'s blue glow, chimney smoke
or *Berghaus* dummy: muffling good mornings
through zipped-up layers of Gore-Tex and wool.

The weir's white noise was my rock n'roll;
rose and fell with the flow and one night
coughed up a tree that stuck to its palate
for seven weeks, changing my lullaby

that winter, that bloody winter.

SUNDERING

There are no rules but your own
and these are open to negotiation.

Not thinking helps but is, rather,
in the spirit of the game than a rule as such.

Not looking is both advisable and covered
by rules 1a through to 3c. High-speed

internet access and misuse of social media
are strongly discouraged (*see: Rule Nine*).

Under the laws of the game, that which was close
flips to the wrong end of your telescope.

Each dawn sees you bury the corpse
only to dig it up again at midnight; this

is purely at the discretion of the arbiter.
One of the players will walk away without looking back,

carrying their grief, like St. Christopher, to the other side.
The other will stumble from one memory to another,

blinding themself in the sharp light of flashback.
Whilst this is not legislated for, it is permitted

under the general code of participant conduct.
What you must understand is that

the rules are not here to ensure fair play,
but a way out of this mess.

ON AN AFTERNOON LIKE THIS SHE TAKES A NEW LOVER

This afternoon you meet your new lover.
I'm in the outfield waiting on catches
while you smile and give back his gaze.
I bend to dry my palms in the June dust
as you raise your glass beside a canal.
I cross to the other side of the square.
You note that he is left-handed, like me.
As you sidestep the man-trap of memory,
I revive an old Scott Walker song.

A wagtail threads its flight-path left to right
in the seconds his hand lingers on your leg.
And as you watch him walk into the pub
you make your decision, while measuring
his length for the cabin bed. In my head
you are nowhere as the ball arcs skyward
and swirls my way. Steadying ourselves,
we prepare for the afternoon's moment.
This says I will drop it. This says he will fit.

UNFOLLOW

The smallest increment, I'm more aware
than know it, but sense some body heat
fall away from the room. Only later

will I check and, sure enough, it is you
who has left; this capture of your days
slipping from a cage which does

not exist but for pel and byte.
The kernel of a thumbnail, small movement
through your fields, the failing pulse

of that broken animal we now are.
We've become contemporary, my love,
succumbed to the typical and the sane.

SMALL LIGHTNINGS

Driving the A4 to Burghclere, last summer
passes me in an ambulance

on the opposite side. The flashing lights
tell me all I need to know: our time

here is taking its leave on a gurney;
worked at by paramedics whose

urgency is slipping with each
failed shock. I do as Dave says

and stand clear. In doing so I see
she looks very much like you

as you slept through your fever,
those three December days in my room.

When you finally came to, you smiled
and pulled me on top of you. Though now,

it's not looking so good for last summer.
I glimpse your tattoo on her shoulder

as he bends over to massage
the pale ribcage. This year

there is no give back of lightning.
Dave I say, *we're losing her.*

ADAM'S GRAVE

Your car shushes the valley floor,
clears its throat on the gravel
and stops beside me.
Doors open.
You and I judge distances;
these days those are fine calculations.
You're wearing that watch I gifted you:
the time I couldn't have
to make this work
properly.

A hill family,
we climb to Adam's Grave to watch the light
fail slowly over Pewsey Vale.
Pronouns fuse in the hill-top gale
and we are a tribe again,
hunting the now for a pelt of future history,
slung across pixels captured digitally.
You pan from your boy to me
and back again
as he tests the incline
himself no longer sure,
waiting for me
to model a gravity.
Together we tumble
and the shutter clicks
trapping the failed light.

THE RIGHT STUFF

Mum got home to find you Googling porn:
mortified and dumb, you'd have none of it.
Don't be too put out, this new test rocket
stands on a launch-pad concrete with love:
a mother's selfless universe of you,
my come-lately pun on fatherhood and
that weird force of tenderness at your core.

Now the countdown has begun, take a seat,
make yourself easy. At twelve you're yet
a space monkey, pawing at the controls
of crude orbit. For some it stays that way,
but you, I think, will graduate to missions
bold with case: stars collapsing into doubt,
strange gravities of bliss, rapture's nebulae.

INKLING

I got airborne late for these times:
at twenty-one on a freebie to Lourdes,
the town where a mother prayed
for my existence. As the plane eased
its butter-knife through the thick pat
of cloud, I remember thinking about
Shakespeare, Dickens, Donne and Hardy.
How they lived their whole lives not seeing
this, except in some flight of fancy.

Likewise my mother, prayer answered,
could not but stow her baggage
in the overhead locker of the brain,
while she tried to conjure the same
cloudy image I see now. You turn
an already familiar face toward
the ultrasound's pen, re-drawing
yourself as fishbone, heartbeat,
the opening sequence from *Doctor Who*.

An extra-terrestrial hand goes to mouth
while the other mimics your mother
and lays across your chest. Already,
your tongue is working away at her,
or are they the words I shall teach you?
Do you have any idea?

LUNG JAZZ

Rocking you in *Costa*
          I see it start to riff;
vowels mainly,
in that scat style of a six-month.

          Improvised as Chet Baker,
soloed like Coltrane,
you try them on for size,
          eyes narrowed, mouth freestyle
lost in your self-jazz.

Consonants are to be wary of,
          not trusted
or finished
                    set aside for later.

Take up the buggy's push-and-pull,
count out   a pause
and discover
the wild love of your own two hands.

Fionn, keep the beat
          and, in your own good time,
tell me what I have lost.